DORSET LEGACY
IN IRON AND STONE

Michael Russell Wood

Aley

First published in 2011 by John Aley, Bridport, Dorset.

ISBN 978-0-9526329-1-7

© Michael Russell Wood 2011

British Library Cataloguing in Publication Data.
A catalogue record for this book is available from the
British Library

Design Luke Murray

Printed by ADP Dorchester, Dorset

CONTENTS

1

King Charles II and The Duke of Monmouth

THE WEST OF DORSET, particularly the Bridport area, is important in the story of King Charles II's escape after his defeat at the battle of Worcester on 3rd September 1651. Charles had returned from exile in France forming an alliance with the Scots to help him gain the throne that was rightfully his.

The Scots were thoroughly beaten by the Parliamentarians at the battle of Dunbar and Oliver Cromwell's New Model Army thrashed the remains of Charles's ill-equipped force at Worcester. A price of £1,000 was put on his head with almost certain death for anyone who helped him.

He had many adventures on his way south to find a boat that would take him to France. His supporters, being Catholic, had over the previous ninety years become well versed in hiding people having been severely persecuted for their religious faith. His first hiding place in Dorset was at Trent, north of Sherborne, at the house of Colonel Wyndham in which there was, and still is, a secret room.

On September 23rd he came down to Charmouth seeking a boat for France but was unsuccessful. He was spotted and Captain Macey with a troop of Roundhead soldiers set out to capture him. Charles was leaving as Macey came rushing into Bridport.

Charles II was probably drinking here in Bridport when he heard that Captain Macey and his troop of Roundhead soldiers were pursuing him.

Charles II turned north here down Lee Lane while his pursuers rushed on towards Dorchester.

Just east of Bridport he turned north down Lee Lane just as his pursuers came rushing by heading eastwards towards Dorchester escaping by the skin of his teeth. He spent the night in Broadwindsor at another tavern, that is now a private house. The next day he went back to hide again at Trent. He eventually managed to leave for France from Brighton on 16th October, six weeks after his defeat at Worcester.

Nine years later Charles was able to return to reclaim his rightful throne but in the meantime he had fathered several children, among them James whose mother Lucy Walter was one of his mistresses. James was created Duke of Monmouth soon after his father's return to the throne. Monmouth was always a Protestant whereas his father and uncle James were Catholics.

KING CHARLES II.

SLEPT HERE

SEPTEMBER 23-24.1651.

ERECTED APRIL 4.1902.

After eluding the troops hunting him Charles II spent the night in Broadwindsor at the George Inn, now a private house, before returning to hide at Trent.

In the church at Longburton is a sign that celebrates the restoration of Charles II as king.

Monmouth had become an experienced soldier during his father's reign although he had spent some of it in exile in Europe. He did have a high opinion of both his own ability and his popularity with the English people. After his father's death and the enthronement of James he decided to return to England to claim the throne for himself. He felt that as a Protestant he would be swept to power.

He landed at Lyme Regis with a small body of men but soon gathered support from the surrounding countryside and it seemed that he would have no trouble claiming the throne. But when his poorly equipped force, nicknamed 'The Pitchfork Rebellion', encountered James II's army at Sedgemoor they were routed.

Monmouth escaped with his life and made his way with a small group of supporters across country to Woodyates where they separated. Monmouth headed over Cranborne Chase towards the South Coast hoping to find a boat at Poole to take him out of the country.

Hungry, cold and alone, with only a dry pea in his pocket, Monmouth was captured under an ash tree near Horton Heath. Although the original ash tree has disappeared, an old ash tree in the spot where he was captured still stands and is known as The Monmouth Ash.

Monmouth was held in Ringwood before being taken to London and beheaded eight days after his capture. His supporters were cruelly treated with over three hundred of them being tried and executed at Judge Jeffreys 'Bloody Assizes' in Dorchester.

The Monmouth Ash, near Horton, where The Duke of Monmouth was captured cold, wet and hungry. Eight days later he was beheaded.

The brass plate marking the Monmouth Ash.

One of Monmouth's supporters who did survive was James Daniel from Beaminster. He was an attorney and a man of property with very strong nonconformist beliefs. He had fought for Monmouth at Sedgemoor and after the battle managed to return to Beaminster. A price was put on his head and capture by King James's troops must have seemed inevitable. After praying for guidance he deemed it wise to escape towards the West.

He hid in a barn at Knowle, between Beaminster and Stoke Abbot. No sooner had he secreted himself under the straw that was stored there than his pursuers arrived. They had been told in

The gate of the Knowle Farm burial ground where James Daniel's remains are interred.

Beaminster that this was a likely hiding place. Despite stabbing the straw with their swords and searching every nook and cranny they failed to discover him and left frustrated.

After his miraculous escape, James Daniel decided that henceforth the barn should be used as a graveyard for him and his family. He returned to his home in Beaminster, the threat of capture having eased, where he lived to the ripe old age of one hundred years.

James Daniel's grave is the flat stone nearest to the hedge.
Opposite: This marble plaque in Beaminster Museum, formerly the Congregational Chapel, celebrates the life and miraculous escape of James Daniel after the Battle of Sedgemoor.

SACRED TO THE MEMORY OF
JAMES DANIEL, GENT.
AN ANCIENT INHABITANT OF THIS TOWN, AND LONG DISTINGUISHED FOR HIS
CHRISTIAN CHARACTER — HIS PROTESTANT NONCONFORMITY — AND HIS
ZEALOUS DEVOTION TO THE CAUSE OF CIVIL AND RELIGIOUS FREEDOM,
UNDER THE TYRANNY OF KING JAMES THE SECOND,
HE ENDURED MUCH DISQUIETUDE FOR CONSCIENCE SAKE, AND ON ONE OCCASION
NARROWLY ESCAPED FALLING INTO THE HANDS OF THE GOVERNMENT
EMISSARIES WHO WERE APPOINTED TO APPREHEND HIM.

THE BURIAL GROUND, ON THE FAMILY ESTATE IN THIS NEIGHBOURHOOD,
AND IN WHICH HIS REMAINS, AND THOSE OF HIS DESCENDANTS ARE INTERRED,
WAS DESIGNED BY HIM TO INDICATE THE PLACE,
AND COMMEMORATE THE EVENT, OF HIS WONDERFUL CONCEALMENT.

HE DIED IN THE YEAR OF OUR LORD, 1711,
AGED ONE HUNDRED YEARS.

HIS SURVIVING RELATIVES,
OF THE FOURTH, FIFTH, SIXTH, AND SEVENTH GENERATIONS,
HAVE UNITED TO REAR THIS TABLET,
IN HONOUR OF THE PIETY AND PRINCIPLES
OF THEIR PATRIARCHAL ANCESTOR.

1835.

TEMPORA MUTANTUR.

2

Two Tragedies on Portland

IT WAS NOT UNTIL 1839 that a bridge was built over the entrance to The Fleet. This connected Portland to the mainland by road; before then it had been necessary to cross the Fleet by ferry. Portlanders had always been very independent and had some customs that seem slightly bizarre to us today. A couple did not marry until the woman became pregnant; she was considered virginal until this happened. Interbreeding was common owing to the closed society of the island, but Charles Wesley, who converted the islanders to Methodism when he preached on Portland in 1746, spoke vehemently against this practice.

Opposite: St George's Church, Reforne, Portland, where the gravestones of William Lano and Mary Way may be found. Their epitaphs tell the tale of the independence and bravery of the Portlanders.

Over two thousand bodies are buried in the graveyard of St George's Church at Easton on The Isle of Portland, many of the gravestones detailing the sad ends to the lives they commemorate. There are many who died in shipwrecks and while saving lives from those wrecks, by accident in the quarries and by being accidentally shot, not to mention the Assistant Chief Warder at Portland Prison who was murdered by a convict, or those who died when their houses collapsed on them during a great storm. But the most tragic story is that of the death of Mary Way together with William Lano.

On 1st April 1803, as the Napoleonic wars were nearing a climax, the frigate HMS Aigle anchored just off Portland Castle. Armed with 36 eighteen pounder cannon, HMS Aigle had been built at Buckler's Hard in 1801, and the next year was commissioned in Plymouth and commanded by George Wolfe Esq. He was a man very reminiscent of Patrick O'Brian's Jack Aubrey, a hard man but an excellent seaman. HMS Aigle had already had a successful cruise capturing two French West Indiamen loaded with coffee, brandy and wine before coming to Portland to impress men for crew. The press gangs had the power to seize men, in fact to kidnap them, to serve in the Royal Navy.

At 5 o'clock on 2nd April, the impress boat from HMS Aigle landed near Portland Castle with the captain, three other officers, a lieutenant of marines with 24 marines and a number of seamen armed with muskets, bayonets, pistols and cutlasses.

They impressed two men in Chiswell and sent them under guard to the Castle and then went on up the hill towards Easton.

Near the church Zach White, the chief constable of the island's Court Leet, asked the impress party what they were doing and they asked for his help. He asked by what authority they were there and Captain Wolfe took out a warrant signed by the mayor of Weymouth. Zach White told him that Weymouth had no jurisdiction since Portland was a Royal Manor owing allegiance directly to the king and he must get a warrant from the county magistrate. Captain Wolfe ignored him continuing into Easton with the press gang.

The islanders who were gathered in Reforne Street reacted violently when the press gang took Robert Bennett captive and a melee ensued in which Captain Wolfe was seized and John Manning, the quartermaster's mate, had his cutlass broken while protecting his captain. A pistol was fired and, to secure their retreat to the Castle, the marines opened fire killing four islanders and wounding others. Particularly badly wounded was twenty-one year old Mary Way who was shot from behind, the bullet passing through her back and lodging in her left breast. She died after seven weeks of agony on 21st May. Despite all this only two islanders were taken by the press gang.

An inquisition was held and the coroner's verdict was of 'wilful murder against the whole', leaving the law to discriminate the ringleaders.

Meanwhile Captain Wolfe sent Lieutenant Hastings and Midshipman John Morgan to Weymouth to inform the Admiralty of the true facts. As they came ashore at Weymouth they were arrested and committed to Dorchester prison, charged

The gravestone of Mary Way in the burial ground of St George's Church, Reforne, Portland. The lettering clearly visible telling the tragic story.

William Lano's gravestone, not so easily legible, tells of the feelings of the Portlanders: *Sacred to the Memory of William Lano, who was wantonly shot by some of a press gang and died of the wound on the 2nd April 1803, Aged 26 years. As over my grave some sorrowing comrade stands / And mourns my fate, cut off by cruel hands / As fancy views I fall upon the ground / And life's warm current running from the wound / Let him explain with poignant grief oppresst / Here unoffending murder'd Victim rests / Oh may my fate in warning accents show / Wat mischief from ungoverned passions flow.*

with murder. Later the names of Captain Wolfe and Marine Lieutenant Jefferies were added to the indictment and the four men were tried at Dorchester Assizes. The evidence from the four accused was that they were being attacked by a mob of over three hundred Portlanders and they had to defend themselves. The jury agreed that they had been acting in self defence and they were all acquitted, much to the disgust of the Portlanders.

*   *   *

Another tragedy that occurred much more recently was the loss of twenty-nine young lives in Portland harbour. On Sunday 17th October 1948 many of the crew of HMS Illustrious, a 23,000 ton aircraft carrier, had enjoyed a day of shore leave rounding it off with an evening in the bars and pubs of Weymouth. Many of them were young men doing their two years of National Service; they boarded the pinnace at around ten o'clock to take them from Weymouth quay back to their ship in Portland harbour.

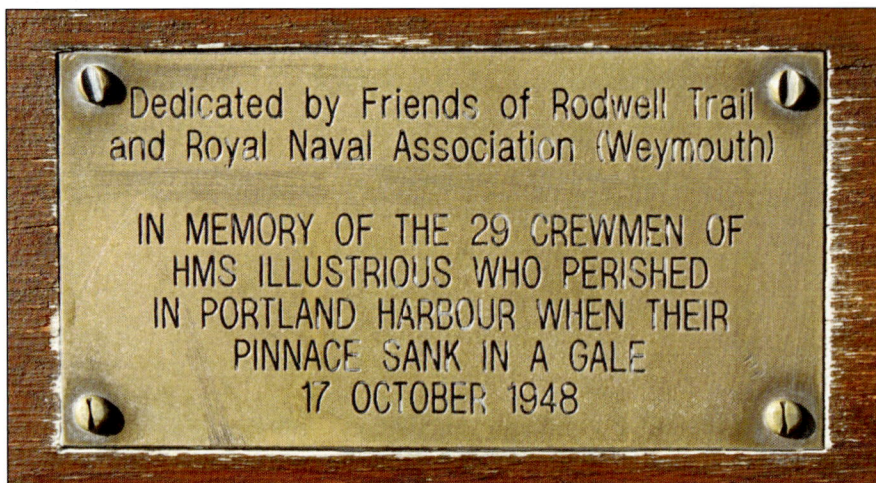

Dedicated by Friends of Rodwell Trail and Royal Naval Association (Weymouth)

IN MEMORY OF THE 29 CREWMEN OF HMS ILLUSTRIOUS WHO PERISHED IN PORTLAND HARBOUR WHEN THEIR PINNACE SANK IN A GALE 17 OCTOBER 1948

A bench overlooking Portland harbour on the Rodwell Trail commemorates the tragedy.

In command of the pinnace was eighteen year old Midshipman Richard Clough. All went well until they turned into Portland harbour where the sea was very rough and the wind strong with driving rain. Although the pinnace had canvas canopies for protection, these were ripped off by the gale and she started to ship water. All the sailors on board were bailing with caps, buckets and anything else they could find.

About fifty yards from HMS Illustrious the pinnace foundered throwing all the sailors into the cold rough sea. The searchlights from the aircraft carrier illuminated the area as frantic efforts were made to rescue any survivors. Some managed to swim to the ship while others were picked up by rescue craft. Of the fifty sailors on board the pinnace only twenty-one survived. Eighteen of those who perished were buried in Portland Naval Cemetery with full military honours.

This memorial was dedicated at Portland Marina in October 2010. It names all those drowned in the HMS Illustrious Tragedy.

3

Six Dorset V.C.s

IN 1856 QUEEN VICTORIA instituted an award for "...most conspicuous bravery, or some daring or pre-eminent act of valour or self sacrifice, or extreme devotion to duty in the presence of the enemy". It was named the Victoria Cross and was the first award for gallantry that could be won by any rank regardless of birth or class. Before then it was only officers whose exceptional bravery was recognised by the award of The Order of the Bath or Mentioned in Despatches.

The Victoria Cross is still the highest award for gallantry in the military services while the George Cross is the equivalent civilian medal.

The Naval Cemetery at Portland, overlooked by the grim Verne Citadel, is the last resting place of many heroes.

Philip Salkeld was the seventh child of The Reverend Robert Salkeld, vicar of the parish of Fontmell Magna. In 1848 at the age of eighteen he joined the Bengal Army but his military career cannot have been stellar since by 1857 he had only risen to the rank of lieutenant in the Bengal Engineers.

In May of 1857 native soldiers of the Bengal Army shot their British officers and marched on Delhi. The Indian Mutiny gathered momentum and the British struggled to maintain control. The mutineers commanded the Fortress of Delhi but on 14th September 1857 Philip Salkeld with a party of three in broad daylight succeeded, under heavy fire, in blowing in the Cashmere Gate and thus ending the siege of the Fortress.

He died a month later from wounds he received at the time. For this brave action he was awarded the Victoria Cross.

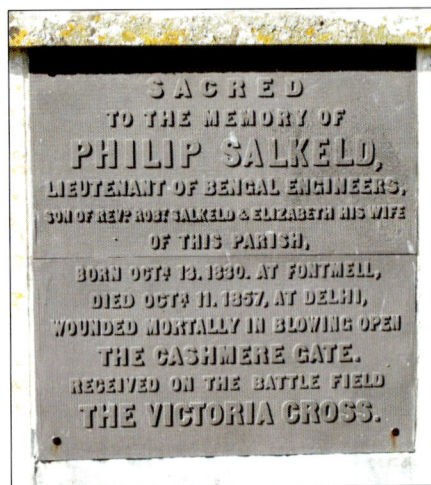

Two faces of the memorial to Philip Salkeld VC in Fontmell Magna churchyard.

Philip Salkeld VC is buried in Delhi but is remembered with a memorial in Fontmell Magna churchyard. His father who was vicar of Fontmell Magna for 46 years is reputedly buried under the memorial to his son.

The memorial to Philip Salkeld VC in Fontmell Magna churchyard.

Reginald Clare Hart was another sapper who was awarded the Victoria Cross on the Indian sub-continent. In 1879 the Second Anglo-Afghan War was raging and on 31st January Lieutenant Hart was on convoy duty near Dakkah when they were attacked by a large force of Afghans with heavy firepower. A Sowar of 13th Bengal Lancers fell wounded 1,200 yards from Lieutenant Hart who immediately ran to protect him, drove off his assailants and, with some assistance, carried the man to cover.

During the entire time, he was exposed to rifle fire from both the river banks and from some enemy in the riverbed. For this act of outstanding bravery he was awarded the Victoria Cross.

Reginald Hart went on to have a distinguished military career ending up as a major-general. He also received recognition for other acts of bravery including saving a life from drowning in Boulogne in 1869 and a gunner from The Ganges Canal, Roorkee, in 1884.

The gravestone of Reginald Clare Hart VC in Netherbury churchyard.

The Second Anglo-Boer war in South Africa is not a conflict that is much mentioned nowadays. The Boers, Dutch settlers, would not submit to British domination; they fought a guerilla campaign but were eventually subdued by a scorched earth policy. It is not a shining episode in British colonial history but some amazing acts of bravery were performed.

On 21st August 1900 Corporal James Knight, a twenty-two year old who had enlisted at the age of fourteen as a bandboy, was with four men covering the rear of Captain Ewart's detachment of Mounted Infantry during a skirmish at Van Wyk's Vlei. His small party were attacked by about fifty enemy but Corporal Knight held his position and after an hour, having lost two of his men, withdrew carrying one wounded companion for nearly two miles. His party were being severely harassed by the enemy as they retreated.

James Huntley Knight's memorial in Milborne St Andrew churchyard.

He was awarded the Victoria Cross for his brave actions and it was presented to him by Lord Kitchener at Pretoria.

After nineteen years he left the army but re-engaged at the outbreak of the Great War. He was rapidly promoted to Regimental Sergeant-Major then commissioned, being promoted to Captain by May 1915. Later that year he resigned his commission and re-enlisted as a Private soldier. He was wounded on The Somme in 1916 and discharged in 1917. He did not die until 1955 and he is remembered in Milborne St Andrew where he had passed the rest of his life.

*   *   *

The first VC awarded to an airman was made to William Rhodes Moorhouse posthumously in April 1915. He had always been a keen flyer having built his own aircraft, the Radley-Moorhouse monoplane, as well as competing in air races both here and in the United States, even flying through the arch of the Golden Gate Bridge in San Francisco. Another of his achievements was to pilot the first passenger flight across the English Channel to France taking his wife and a newspaper reporter.

At the start of the Great War, Moorhouse joined the Royal Flying Corps and was soon in France at Merville with No 2 Squadron equipped with BE2b aircraft. The BE2b was a very slow but stable aircraft. Designed in 1912 and built by the Royal Aircraft Factory, it had a maximum speed of 70mph. Don't forget this was only nine years after the first ever powered flight. It was known to the Germans as 'Kaltes Fleisch' (cold meat), and to the pilots of the Royal Flying Corps by a number of less than complimentary names.

A partially assembled replica of a BE2b at Old Sarum airfield, the type of aircraft flown by Rhodes Moorhouse.

On 26th April 1915 he was briefed to drop a 100lb bomb, the largest that the BE2b could carry, on the railway junction at Courtrai. Descending to 300ft, Moorhouse dropped his bomb accurately on the target but was met by a barrage of small arms and machine gun fire that ripped open his thigh and severely damaged his aircraft.

He descended to about 100ft to increase his airspeed but this made him more vulnerable to machine gun fire and he was hit again in the abdomen. Nevertheless, although mortally wounded, Moorhouse managed to nurse his plane the thirty five miles back to Merville and make a perfect landing. Lifted from the aircraft he insisted on being de-briefed before being taken to the casualty station where he died the next day.

A sad sequel to this story of heroism is that Rhodes Moorhouse's son, also William, who was born shortly before his father's death, joined the RAF and became a pilot flying a Hurricane with 601 Squadron in The Battle of Britain. He was shot down by a Messerschmitt Bf 109 and perished. He is buried alongside his father near Parnham House which had been the family home.

This plain brass plaque commemorates the bravery of William Rhodes Moorhouse. It has become embedded in a beech tree near the road from Melplash to Beaminster.

In Powerstock churchyard a simple wooden cross, carved with the emblem of the Victoria Cross marks the grave of Victor Crutchley. As a twenty four year old naval lieutenant, he was on HMS Vindictive when, in 1918, the British Navy attempted to block the entrance to Ostend harbour. The first attempt using HMS Vindictive as an assault ship failed with the vessel badly damaged and the harbour still open to the German navy. A second attempt was made using HMS Vindictive as a blockship; both her captain and the navigator were killed on the way in.

Lieutenant Crutchley then took command but she ran aground at the entrance to the channel. Under continuous fire he managed to ensure that the remaining crew of HMS Vindictive and that of ML254, whose captain had collapsed from his wounds, were safely transferred to HMS Warwick.

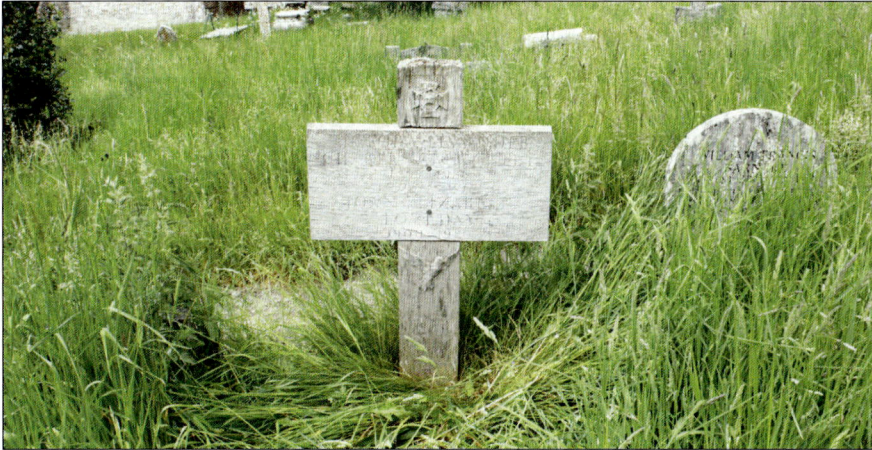

The simple wooden cross that marks Victor Crutchley's grave in Powerstock churchyard. Note the Victoria Cross emblem carved into the upright. This cross was not easy to find since it was almost entirely obscured by long grass and weeds.

This attempt at blocking the channel into Ostend was only partially successful but Lieutenant Crutchley's bravery and seamanship under concentrated enemy gunfire was recognised by the award of the Victoria Cross. After a successful career in the Royal Navy reaching the rank of Admiral he retired in 1947 then devoting his time to his estate in Dorset, being Master of the Cattistock Hunt as well as Deputy Lieutenant and High Sheriff of the county.

I remember seeing him in the late 1950s at the Boxing Day meet of the Cattistock Foxhounds in Bridport. A grand figure in his hunting pink and magnificent beard, he addressed the crowd from a first floor window of The Bull. He was a commanding presence and he always ended his Boxing Day speech with the injunction to 'Shut the gates'. The crowd were waiting for this and joined in lustily. He died on 24th January 1986 at the great age of ninety three years.

*   *   *

Another Victoria Cross awarded to a member of The Royal Navy was that which was awarded posthumously to twenty-three year old Leading Seaman Jack Mantle.

HMS Foylebank had been a 5,000 ton merchant ship, but was converted for use as an anti-aircraft protection vessel. She had been fitted with 2-pounder pom poms, .5" machine guns and four twin 4" turrets.

The Germans were afraid that this vessel could severely hinder their attacks on British shipping. On 4th July 1940 they mounted a concentrated dive bombing raid on Portland Dockyard and especially HMS Foylebank moored there. In eight minutes, the twenty-six Stuka dive bombers had killed one hundred and seventy-six crew out of the total complement of three hundred sailors.

During the attack Jack Mantle continued firing his pom pom anti-aircraft gun; his left leg was shattered by a bomb but he stayed at his post. Undaunted, after the ship's electric power supply had been destroyed, he died from multiple wounds still firing his gun.

An interesting sidelight on these brave men is that of the six whose bravery was recognised by the Victoria Cross, three were awarded it posthumously while the three who survived lived to an average age of eighty four years.

Jack Mantle's grave in the Naval Cemetery at Portland overlooking the dockyard where he died so bravely for his country defending HMS Foylebank against a German dive bomber attack.

4

The Chideock Martyrs

JUST A FEW HUNDRED YARDS from the main A35 road, as it passes through Chideock, is the place where Chideock Castle stood. You can walk up Ruins Lane and through the gate into the field, up over the grass to where a tall cross stands and the village is laid out before you with the sea in the distance.

It was in 1951 that Lt. Col. Humphrey Weld of the Chideock Estate owned by his forbears erected the memorial to the Chideock Martyrs on the site of the ruins of Chideock Castle.

Opposite: The view over the village towards the sea from the memorial to the Chideock Martyrs on the site of the ruins of the Castle.

In the 16th century anyone professing or practising the Roman Catholic Faith was considered to be an enemy and traitor since France and Spain, our enemies, were strongly Catholic. They were liable to be punished by death unless they renounced the Catholic Faith. This had followed the Reformation of the English church when Henry VIII broke away from the church of Rome.

The brass plaque on the Chideock Martyrs Memorial the wording of which reads: *The Martyrs' Cross On this spot stood Chideock Castle built by Sir John de Chideocke in 1380, it was taken and destroyed by Parliamentary forces in 1645. During the reigns of Elizabeth I and Charles I five men went out from here to die for their Catholic Faith. This cross is dedicated to their memory and two other martyrs from Chideock who also died for their faith. John Cornelius, Thomas Bosgrave, Patrick Salmon, John Carey, Hugh Green, William Pike and Thomas Pilchard.*

The Arundells, who lived at Chideock Castle, were Catholics not brandishing their faith but nevertheless had their own personal chaplain whom they kept concealed. One of these, John Cornelius, chaplain to Lady Arundell, was betrayed by a servant. He was arrested by the Sheriff of Dorset in April 1594. As he was being taken away bare headed, Thomas Bosgrave offered him his own hat whereupon he was also arrested together with two servants John Carey and Patrick Salmon.

Cornelius was taken to London and questioned in front of both the Lord Treasurer and the Archbishop of Canterbury. Despite torture he would not reveal the name of anyone who had given him help or shelter, nor would he renounce his Faith.

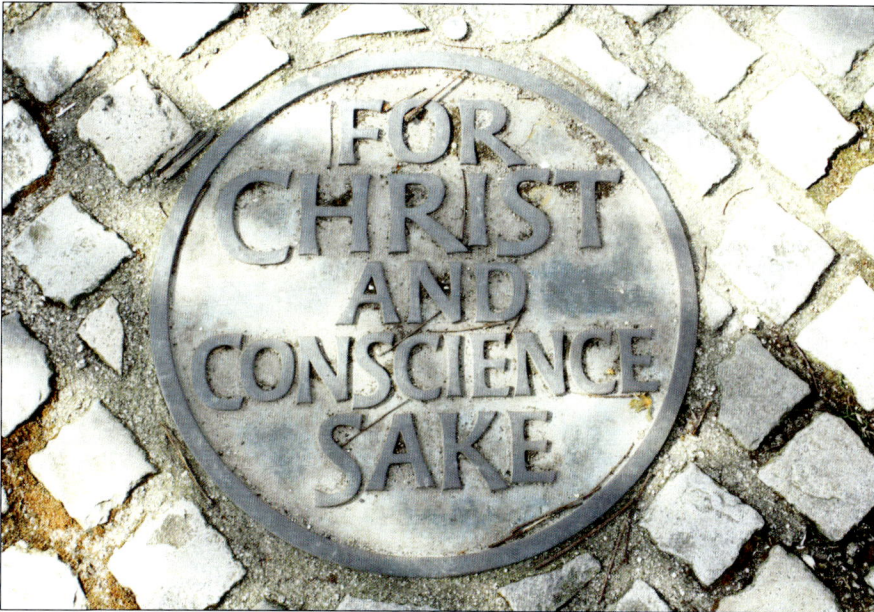

The site where the Dorchester gallows stood, at the end of South Walks, Dorchester.

He was taken back to Dorchester where, on 2nd July, he was condemned to death. He was accused of High Treason since he was a priest and the others were charged with felony since they had helped him, knowing him to be a priest.

They were offered a pardon if they would renounce their Faith but they went to the gallows with dignity. On 4th July they died, each one showing no signs of fear and proclaiming their beliefs till the end.

The statues commemorating the Dorchester and Chideock Martyrs, by Elizabeth Frink, in South Walks, Dorchester. The hangman is facing two of his victims.

In those days hanging was a particularly unpleasant death. The body was hung from the gallows, not dropped to break the neck, and while the victim was still conscious he was cut open and the heart removed. The body was then cut into four and the head nailed to the gibbet or kicked around like a football by the Dorchester Puritans.

Some years before this Fr Thomas Pilchard, another chaplain at Chideock Castle, had been executed together with one of his converts, William Pike.

Blessed Hugh Green was another chaplain at the Castle. In 1641 King Charles I, in an effort to placate the Puritans, issued a proclamation banishing all Catholic priests. Green was arrested, tried, and condemned to death. The executioner was quite unskilled in his gruesome profession and was unable to find Green's heart. This appalling cruelty continued for nearly half an hour until he finally died.

*   *   *

In the Roman Catholic country of France, in 1598, Henry IV issued the Edict of Nantes that gave rights to Protestant Huguenots and allowed them 'Freedom of Conscience'. But nearly 100 years later Louis XIV renounced this Edict. This precipitated a mass exodus of Huguenots from France many of whom came to England.

The daughter of one of these refugees is commemorated in Little Bredy church. Her epitaph clearly shows that she was thought of as a fine character.

Now that we live in a secular society it is sometimes difficult to visualise the passions that religious beliefs can engender. But think of Ireland. The cruelty there has been indiscriminate but not official policy.

In the sixteenth and seventeenth centuries, although persecution of Catholics was the official policy it was limited to specific people; nevertheless, in England during the 146 years between 1535 and 1681, about 360 men and women died for their Catholic Faith.

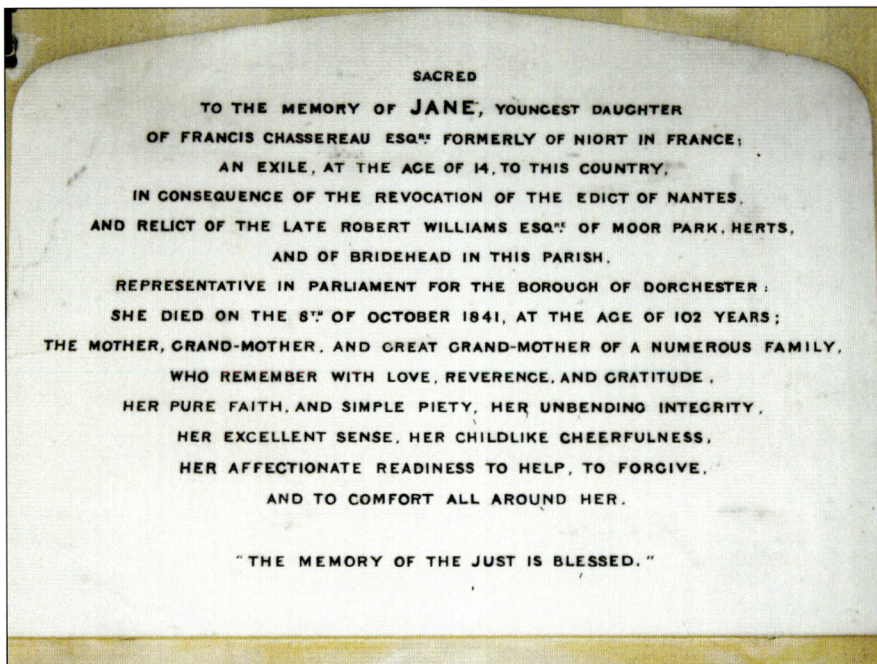

SACRED

TO THE MEMORY OF JANE, YOUNGEST DAUGHTER
OF FRANCIS CHASSEREAU ESQ.RE FORMERLY OF NIORT IN FRANCE;
AN EXILE, AT THE AGE OF 14, TO THIS COUNTRY,
IN CONSEQUENCE OF THE REVOCATION OF THE EDICT OF NANTES.
AND RELICT OF THE LATE ROBERT WILLIAMS ESQ.RE OF MOOR PARK, HERTS,
AND OF BRIDEHEAD IN THIS PARISH,
REPRESENTATIVE IN PARLIAMENT FOR THE BOROUGH OF DORCHESTER :
SHE DIED ON THE 8TH OF OCTOBER 1841, AT THE AGE OF 102 YEARS;
THE MOTHER, GRAND-MOTHER, AND GREAT GRAND-MOTHER OF A NUMEROUS FAMILY,
WHO REMEMBER WITH LOVE, REVERENCE, AND GRATITUDE,
HER PURE FAITH, AND SIMPLE PIETY, HER UNBENDING INTEGRITY,
HER EXCELLENT SENSE, HER CHILDLIKE CHEERFULNESS,
HER AFFECTIONATE READINESS TO HELP, TO FORGIVE,
AND TO COMFORT ALL AROUND HER.

"THE MEMORY OF THE JUST IS BLESSED."

The epitaph of Jane Williams in Little Bredy church. Her father was a refugee from the persecution of Protestants in France.
Opposite: Detail of the hangman by Elizabeth Frink in South Walks, Dorchester.

5

Some Dorset Heroes

EDWARD JENNER IS KNOWN AS 'The Father of Smallpox Vaccination' but in Worth Matravers churchyard is the grave of a man who successfully vaccinated his family against smallpox twenty years before Jenner first immunised anyone against the disease. He is Benjamin Jesty.

In 1774 when he was farming at Yetminster a smallpox epidemic was raging. This very infectious disease was often fatal, but Jesty had noticed that dairy girls who had suffered from cowpox never seemed to contract smallpox; ergo, he thought, this protected them from smallpox.

He bravely infected his family with cowpox by scratching the skin on their arms and putting pus from the udder of a cowpox infected cow on the wounds. The cowpox ran its course in his family; although his wife had a fever for a few days they all totally recovered. This gave them lifelong protection from smallpox.

Jesty and his family were reviled locally, many saying that they would turn into cows or grow horns. He rose above this scorn probably secretly vaccinating other people. Later, when he had moved to Worth Matravers, he is known to have carried out several vaccinations.

Benjamin Jesty's grave in Worth Matravers Churchyard.

In 1805 Benjamin Jesty was invited to London with his son Robert to attend the 'Original Vaccine Pock Institution'. Robert was publicly infected with live smallpox but remained quite unharmed. This was certified by twelve of the Institute's examining officers and the result published in the Edinburgh Medical and Surgical Journal. The members of the Institute were very impressed by this successful vaccination against smallpox carried out thirty years earlier. As a token of their admiration they commissioned a three quarter length portrait of Benjamin for their building. This painting was recently acquired by The Wellcome Trust.

*   *   *

On the quayside at Weymouth is a bronze plaque that commemorates two brave Dorset men; Richard Clark and John Endicott.

Richard Clark, who was born in Weymouth, was Master of the vessel Delight and in 1583 he sailed from Weymouth joining Sir Humphrey Gilbert's expedition to claim land in America.

Sir Humphrey Gilbert had lived an adventurous life; a fearless soldier he had fought in Ireland and in the Netherlands as well as being a member of parliament. He secured by letters patent the right to seize for the crown nine million acres of land, that was to be let to settlers, in America.

Although this was not a well organised expedition, one vessel turning back because it was short of food, they reached America. With Richard Clark, Gilbert succeeded in claiming Newfoundland for Queen Elizabeth on 5th August 1583.

The plaque commemorating Richard Clark and John Endicott on Weymouth Quay.

Returning across the Atlantic, Gilbert insisted on sailing in the Squirrel rather than the more seaworthy Golden Hind; the Squirrel sank in a storm with all hands. Richard Clark, although being shipwrecked, survived and was able to return to Weymouth and encourage trade with Newfoundland.

John Endicott was born in Dorchester and must have been strongly influenced by the Rev. John White who had extreme puritan views and was very involved in sending Dorset men and women to America so that they could have 'liberty of conscience'. Endicott sailed to America from Weymouth on 20th June 1628 in the vessel Abigail with sixty other men.

Arriving at Naumkeag he established the settlement whose name was later changed to Salem. This name is a corruption of the word shalom meaning peace. An austere Puritan, he was governor of the Massachusetts Bay Colony for many years.

Despite his extreme dislike of Quakers, long hair and women without veils at public assemblies, he apparently dispensed justice fairly. He died, aged about seventy-seven, still in office.

* * *

By the side of the road between Clouds Hill and Bovington is a memorial stone marking the spot where T. E. Lawrence had his fatal motorcycle accident on 19th May 1935. Riding on his Brough Superior SS100 from his cottage at Clouds Hill to post a letter in Bovington Camp, he swerved to avoid two boys in the road, lost control and was fatally injured.

Lawrence was born in 1888 and graduated from Jesus College Oxford with a first class honours degree. Between 1910 and 1914 he worked as an archaeologist in the Middle East, latterly also gathering intelligence for the British military.

On being commissioned into the British army he was sent to the headquarters in Cairo where, with his knowledge of the area and the language, he was soon amongst the Arab tribes uniting them against the Turks.

Towards the end of the Great War, Lawrence tried to convince the government that an independent Arab state was in British interests, but the promises that he had made to the Arab leaders were all broken by the secret Sykes-Picot Agreement. He ended his army service as a Lieutenant-Colonel.

In 1922 after a spell in the Colonial Office Lawrence enlisted in the RAF under the name of Ross, but was discovered and forced to leave. He then joined the Royal Tank Corps having changed his name to Shaw.

The shrine near the place of Lawrence's death.

Detail of the stone marking the place of Lawrence's fatal crash.

Later, he managed to transfer to the RAF where he served till 1935 with the rank of aircraftman. He died less than two months after leaving the RAF at the age of forty-six.

A very clever, brave and complicated man, Lawrence served his country and the Hashemite Arabs with courage and bravery and complete dedication. He wrote several books but the autobiographical 'Seven Pillars of Wisdom' is probably the most important. His portrayal in the 1962 film 'Lawrence of Arabia' gives a good impression of the part he played in the Middle East during the Great War.

The effigy of T.E. Lawrence in St Martin's Church, Wareham, carved by Eric Kennington. This sculpture was refused by Salisbury cathedral but was found a very suitable resting place here.

6

World War II

BUILDING UP TO D-Day the whole American Army 1st Infantry Division was stationed in Dorset to say nothing of the British and other Allied troops.

To avoid trouble between black and white soldiers in Lyme Regis, the pubs were open on alternate days to either coloured or white troops. Corfe Mullen became known as Little Harlem and there, to keep them separate, the only pub that the black soldiers were allowed to go to was The Halfway House on Bournemouth Road.

The memorial in Victoria Gardens Portland, placed by the Americans.

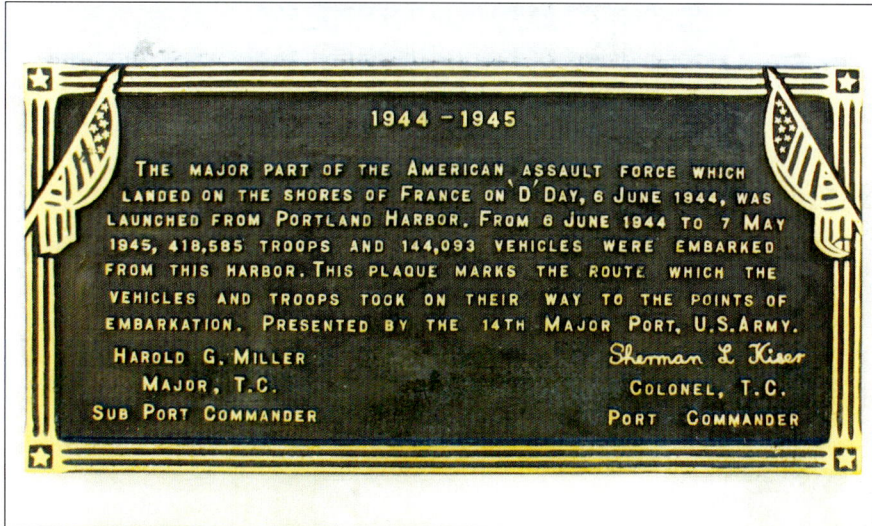

Detail of the plaque in Victoria Gardens, Portland.

On 2nd June 1944 the entire American 1st Division, known as The Big Red One, consisting of 34,142 soldiers and 3,100 vehicles, started to move to their embarkation ports. On the night of 5th June with a break in the weather, the order was given and they departed, starting the liberation of Occupied Europe on 6th June.

Between 5th June 1944 and 7th May 1945, through Portland Harbour alone, 418,585 troops and 144,093 vehicles were embarked for Europe. This remarkable achievement is commemorated in Victoria Gardens on Portland. The return traffic not only brought back wounded Allied troops but also over 35,000 German prisoners of war who were held captive in England for the duration of hostilities.

*   *   *

To the east of Blandford, near the village of Tarrant Rushton, there is a plateau where in 1942 an RAF airfield was established. It had three runways, so the airfield could be used in whatever direction the wind was blowing. This was particularly important for glider towing which initially was one of the main uses of this airfield.

The only remaining evidence of the existence of this airfield is one T2 aircraft hangar and a fine memorial at Windy Corner, on the road from Tarrant Rushton to Witchampton, the site of the main entrance.

Between 1943 and 1944, the main activity on this airfield was the training of glider pilots for heavy military gliders. These gliders named Horsa and Hamilcar were towed behind four-

Windy Corner, once the main entrance to Tarrant Rushton Airfield, the memorial stone with the old T2 hangar in the background.

Two of the plaques on the memorial stone at the old main entrance to Tarrant Rushton airfield.

The third plaque on the memorial stone at the old main entrance to Tarrant Rushton airfield.

engined Handley Page Halifaxes. The Horsa could carry 28 men, a jeep, or other equipment. The Hamilcar was designed to be able to carry a light tank such as the Tetrarch, two bren gun carriers, or 40 troops. Both gliders were constructed mainly from plywood and flown by members of the RAF Glider Pilot Regiment or the Army Air Corps.

These glider pilots and airborne troops were very courageous. They had relatively little training and accidents were not uncommon, with tow ropes breaking and tug aircraft breaking down. Then, when they were released from their tow, hopefully in the right place, they had to try to put the glider down in a hostile environment without damaging their loads.

On D-Day a great armada of gliders loaded with troops and equipment took off from Tarrant Rushton to attack the German positions near Caen and help clear the area for the Allied seaborne landings. The successful operation was also a morale booster for the ground troops that were already fighting there.

Most of the gliders for Operation Market Garden in mid-September 1944 were towed from Tarrant Rushton. This was the allied attempt to cross the Rhine at Arnhem.

The four-engined Halifax aircraft were used for dropping supplies to French resistance groups and Special Operations Executive agents as well as their glider tug duties. The Westland

The nose and part of the fuselage of a Horsa glider at The Museum of Army Flying, Middle Wallop.

Lysander, often used to drop and pick up agents in Occupied Europe, was another aircraft that on occasion flew out of Tarrant Rushton.

After the war Tarrant Rushton was abandoned by the RAF but in 1948 Sir Alan Cobham's Flight Refuelling took it over. The Berlin Airlift had just started and they converted Lancasters and Lancastrians to carry fuel into isolated West Berlin. In one year nearly 4,500 sorties were flown from Tarrant Rushton supplying fuel to West Berlin.

For the next thirty years Flight Refuelling used Tarrant Rushton mainly for converting and developing aircraft for in-flight refuelling. They left the airfield in the 1970s and the airfield closed forever on 30th September 1980.

The Westland Lysander ferried agents to and from Occupied Europe from Tarrant Rushton. This restored example is in The Shuttleworth Collection.

7

Roads and Bridges

A S YOU TRAVEL north from Beaminster towards Mosterton and Crewkerne the road takes you through Beaminster tunnel formerly known as Horn Hill tunnel. This civil engineering project was completed in 1832 taking less than three years from the application for the necessary Act of Parliament. That the construction went so quickly was due in a large part to the efforts of one man – Giles Russell.

Russell was a respected Beaminster attorney who was involved in the Bridport 2nd District Turnpike Trust which controlled the road from Bridport through Beaminster to Misterton where it joined the road from Dorchester to Crewkerne. He was determined to increase the traffic on the Bridport to Crewkerne route for the benefit of local trade.

The inscription on the south portal to Beaminster tunnel.

He never lost his enthusiasm for the construction of the tunnel and was chiefly instrumental in getting the Act of Parliament passed that enabled it to be built. He enthused others and he himself invested £2,000 in the project.

Turnpikes were toll roads controlled by trusts who by law were able to charge for passing along their stretch of road but were also obliged to maintain that road.

The road from Bridport to Crewkerne was important for the transport of flax and hemp to southern Somerset and the west of England. Horn Hill was a barrier to the easy flow of goods and the opening of the tunnel removed this obstacle. The engineer appointed by the Trust to design and supervise the construction was twenty-nine year old Michael Lane. He had been working

The south portal to Beaminster tunnel. The memorial to William Aplin is on the left hand side.

The only death in the construction of Beaminster tunnel was that of William Aplin, killed by a fall of earth.

for Marc Brunel on the Wapping to Rotherhithe Thames tunnel until, in 1828, work stopped due to flooding and shortage of money.

Despite difficulties, particularly with 'wet and running sand', that is now known to geologists as Greensand, Michael Lane completed the work in ten months between August 1831 and June 1832. The tunnel is made from brick with stone portals and apart from routine maintenance nothing serious has had to be done to it since.

Lane went on to do much work on the railways, ending his career as Chief Engineer on the Great Western Railway.

The tunnel opened with great celebrations but within a few years the spread of the railways had started to undermine its commercial importance. In 1881 the Bridport 2nd District Turnpike Trust was wound up as the turnpike era came to an end, but it has left us with a fine tunnel still in continuous use today.

Sadly, the toll house for the tunnel, which was by the north portal, was demolished for a road improvement scheme in 1963, but a particularly fine example of toll house is still to be seen just outside Dorchester on the entrance to what was the turnpike to Maiden Newton and Barwick (Yeovil).

Turnpike trusts were obliged by their constitution to place milestones along their roads but the bridges were the responsibility of the county. Small bridges were the responsibility of the parishes in which they were situated.

A fine example of a toll house just outside Dorchester.

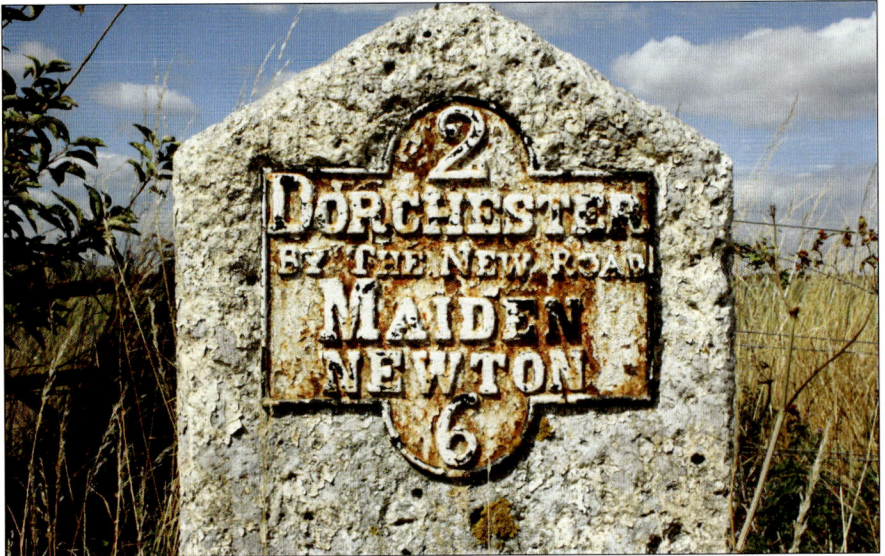

A well preserved milestone on the road between Dorchester and Maiden Newton.

In the centre of Dorchester distances are still clearly marked.

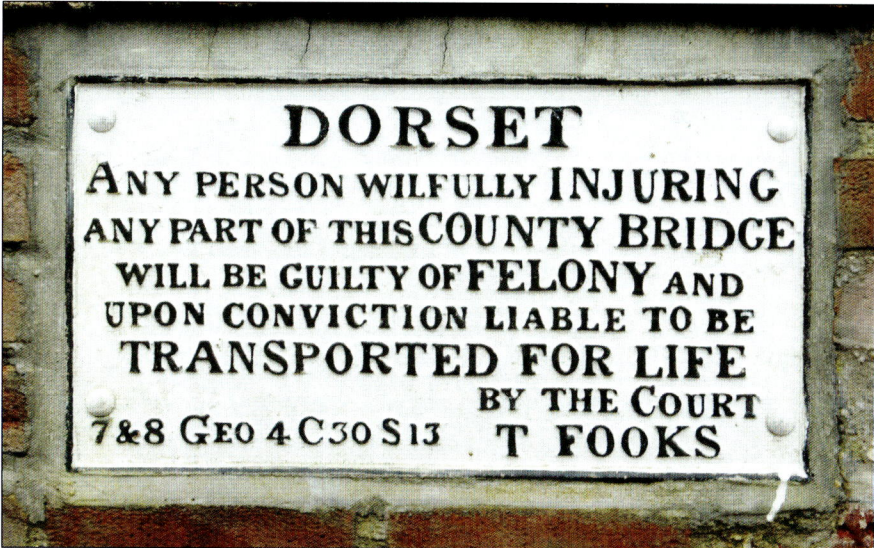

This sign can still be seen on several Dorset bridges but the threat of transportation was never carried out.

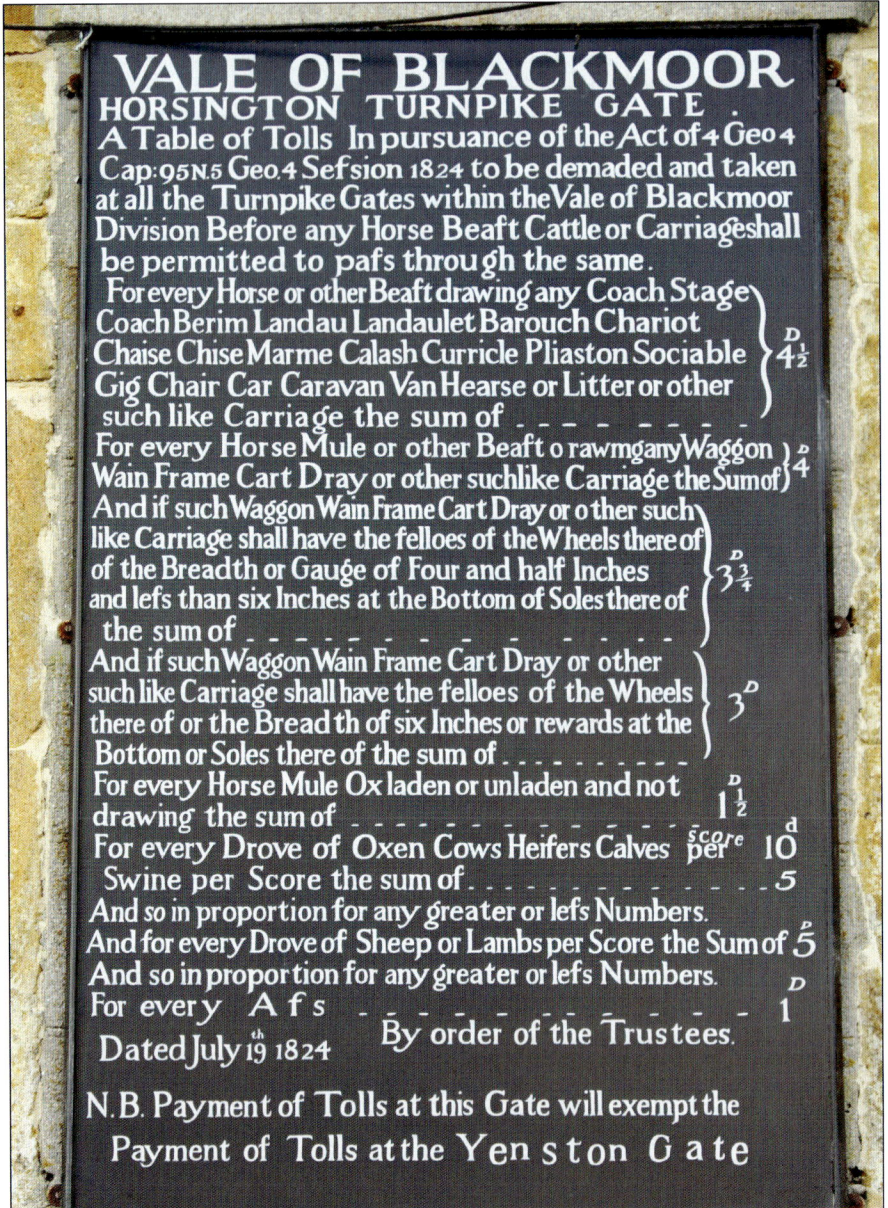

VALE OF BLACKMOOR
HORSINGTON TURNPIKE GATE.

A Table of Tolls In pursuance of the Act of 4 Geo 4 Cap: 95 N.5 Geo.4 Sefsion 1824 to be demaded and taken at all the Turnpike Gates within the Vale of Blackmoor Division Before any Horse Beaft Cattle or Carriage shall be permitted to pafs through the same.

For every Horse or other Beaft drawing any Coach Stage Coach Berim Landau Landaulet Barouch Chariot Chaise Chise Marme Calash Curricle Pliaston Sociable Gig Chair Car Caravan Van Hearse or Litter or other such like Carriage the sum of 4½D

For every Horse Mule or other Beaft o rawmgany Waggon Wain Frame Cart Dray or other suchlike Carriage the Sum of 4D

And if such Waggon Wain Frame Cart Dray or other such like Carriage shall have the felloes of the Wheels there of of the Breadth or Gauge of Four and half Inches and lefs than six Inches at the Bottom of Soles there of the sum of 3¾D

And if such Waggon Wain Frame Cart Dray or other such like Carriage shall have the felloes of the Wheels there of or the Bread th of six Inches or rewards at the Bottom or Soles there of the sum of 3D

For every Horse Mule Ox laden or unladen and not drawing the sum of 1½D

For every Drove of Oxen Cows Heifers Calves per score 10d

Swine per Score the sum of 5

And so in proportion for any greater or lefs Numbers.

And for every Drove of Sheep or Lambs per Score the Sum of 5D

And so in proportion for any greater or lefs Numbers.

For every A f s 1D

Dated July 19th 1824   By order of the Trustees.

N.B. Payment of Tolls at this Gate will exempt the Payment of Tolls at the Yenston Gate

The toll rates at the Horsington gate just over the Somerset border.

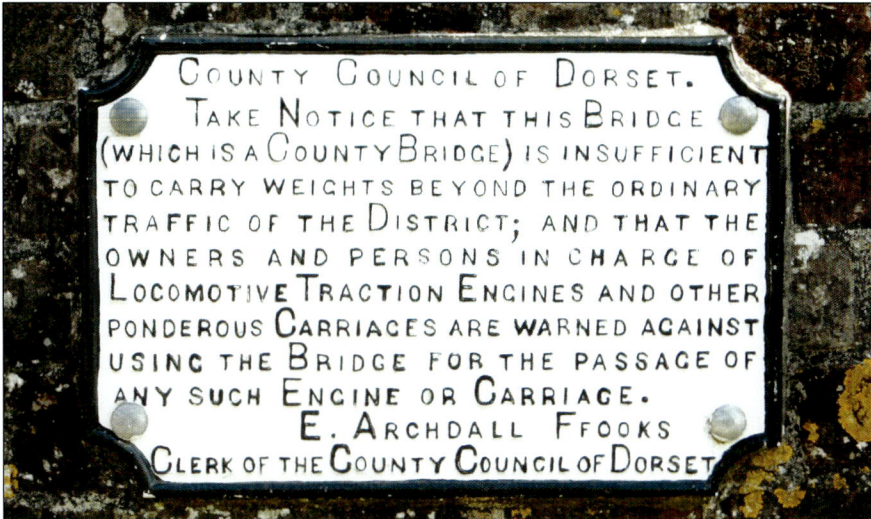

COUNTY COUNCIL OF DORSET.
TAKE NOTICE THAT THIS BRIDGE
(WHICH IS A COUNTY BRIDGE) IS INSUFFICIENT
TO CARRY WEIGHTS BEYOND THE ORDINARY
TRAFFIC OF THE DISTRICT; AND THAT THE
OWNERS AND PERSONS IN CHARGE OF
LOCOMOTIVE TRACTION ENGINES AND OTHER
PONDEROUS CARRIAGES ARE WARNED AGAINST
USING THE BRIDGE FOR THE PASSAGE OF
ANY SUCH ENGINE OR CARRIAGE.
E. ARCHDALL FFOOKS
CLERK OF THE COUNTY COUNCIL OF DORSET

After the turnpikes disappeared, the County Council had sole responsibility for the maintenance of main roads and bridges.

AUTOMOBILE ASSOCIATION
IWERNE MINSTER 4½
TARRANT GUNVILLE
TARRANT HINTON 1½
LONDON 102
SAFETY FIRST

Between the wars, the Automobile Association put up signs in many towns and villages.

The red signpost east of Bere Regis. Perhaps there was a gibbet here or maybe it was a marker for convicts walking to Poole for transportation to Australia.

In Tout Quarry on Portland is a beautiful bridge built in 1854 by J.C. Lano. It is made without any mortar or cement and is still in perfect condition. It was part of the Merchants' Railway, the first private railway in the country and funded jointly by stone merchants to carry stone down to the barges at Castletown. From Castletown, Portland stone was transported by sea to be used for important buildings especially in London.

Lano's Arch in Tout Quarry, Portland.

Detail of the fine stonework of Lano's Arch.

8

The Birth of Trade Unionism

UNTIL THE CONSTRUCTION of the Puddletown By-pass, the A35 road through Tolpuddle had been a continuous stream of traffic both night and day. Now it is peaceful, with only the occasional car or lorry to disturb the peace. But on one day each year thousands of trade union members arrive to remember, with bands and speeches, a seminal event in the history of trade unionism.

Opposite: This sycamore tree is now growing where the Tolpuddle Martyrs used to meet before they were arrested, tried and sentenced to transportation to Australia.

In the early 1830s, farming was not prospering and the conditions of the farm workers trying to live on ten shillings (50p) a week were quite pitiable. In the Tolpuddle area the farmers would only pay nine shillings (45p) a week which they wanted to reduce to six shillings (30p) a week. To try to counter this injustice the Friendly Society of Agricultural Labourers was formed in Tolpuddle. Friendly societies were no longer illegal since the Act banning them had been repealed in 1824.

The leader of this Friendly Society was George Loveless who as well as being a farm labourer was a Methodist Local Preacher. Being a Local Preacher meant that he had been examined by a senior Methodist and was entitled to preach and lead worship but not administer the Sacraments. As well as preaching and leading

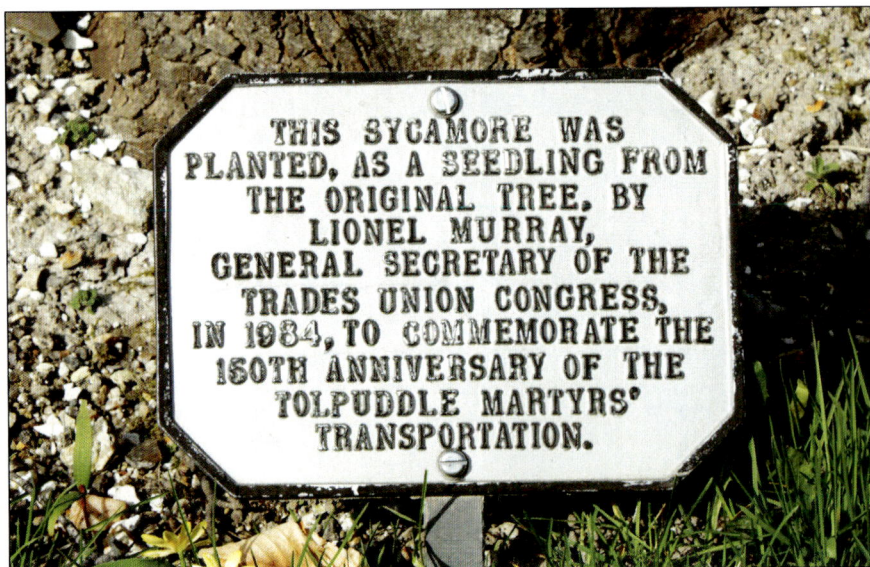

THIS SYCAMORE WAS PLANTED, AS A SEEDLING FROM THE ORIGINAL TREE, BY LIONEL MURRAY, GENERAL SECRETARY OF THE TRADES UNION CONGRESS, IN 1984, TO COMMEMORATE THE 150TH ANNIVERSARY OF THE TOLPUDDLE MARTYRS' TRANSPORTATION.

Len Murray, as well as being General secretary of the TUC, was also a Methodist Local Preacher.

IN THIS BUILDING
ON MARCH 19TH., 1834
THE SIX TOLPUDDLE MARTYRS WERE SENTENCED
TO SEVEN YEARS TRANSPORTATION
FOR THEIR PART IN THE FOUNDING
OF RURAL TRADE UNIONISM
*Unveiled by Alderman E.G.Gooch C.B.E., J.P., M.P.
President of the National Union of Agricultural Workers*
JULY 1947.

This plaque is on the wall of the old Shire Hall in Dorchester where the Tolpuddle Martyrs were tried and sentenced.

services he would have done much pastoral work. Three other members of the Friendly Society were also Local Preachers.

In March 1834, James Brine, James Hammett, George Loveless, James Loveless, Thomas Standfield and John Standfield agreed that they would not work for less than ten shillings a week. While this action of the Friendly Society was legal the members had sworn an oath to each other when they had founded the Society.

When the farmers and local landowners realised that their complete domination of their workers was being challenged they determined to find a way to stop this threat to their total control of the local farm labourers. They invoked an Act of 1797, the Unlawful Oaths Act. This Act, forbidding secret oaths of loyalty or pledges, had been passed to deal with a naval mutiny.

It was now used to bring the six to trial in Dorchester. The six were arrested for unlawful assembly and charged with 'administering unlawful oaths'. During the trial George Loveless said "We have injured no man's reputation, character, person or property. We were uniting together to preserve ourselves, our wives and our children from utter degradation and starvation."

Despite the eloquence and sincerity of George Loveless, the jury, that comprised mainly local landowners and farmers, passed a guilty verdict and under some official pressure the judge sentenced the six men to seven years transportation to the penal colony in New South Wales. This harsh sentence was '...not for anything they had done, but as an example to others'.

The memorial arch of the Methodist Chapel in Tolpuddle.

After the sentence was passed, George Loveless wrote on a scrap of paper these words:

> God is our guide! from field, from wave,
> From plough, from anvil and from loom;
> We come our country's rights to save,
> And speak a tyrant faction's doom;
> We raise the watchword liberty;
> We will, we will, we will be free!

The six men suffered horrifying privations during the voyage to Australia, as did all the convicts being transported, being in irons the whole time. The conditions were no better than a slave trading vessel with less than seven square feet of space per man. In the New South Wales penal colony, they were treated as, or more harshly than, any other convict, but their deep Christian faith and belief in their cause gave them strength.

Meanwhile in England they had become popular heroes and Lord John Russell had become Home Secretary. Part of Lord Russell's argument to the Prime Minister for freeing the six was "...that if being members of a secret society and administering secret oaths was a crime, the reactionary Duke of Cumberland as head of the Orange Lodges was equally deserving of transportation". In 1836 under intense popular pressure they were released with the exception of James Hammett who was set free a year later.

James Hammett returned to Tolpuddle spending the rest of his life there and is buried in Tolpuddle churchyard. He died in 1891 in the Dorchester workhouse. The others went first of all to

The grave of James Hammett in Tolpuddle churchyard. He was the only one of the Martyrs who remained in England.

Essex but soon emigrated to Canada, settling in London, Ontario. There they became respected members of the community and are remembered to this day by a monument in their honour as well as an affordable housing cooperative and trade union complex named after them.

The bravery and determination of these six men has inspired many generations to fight for improved working conditions and a living wage. They fearlessly suffered for their beliefs in liberty and by their actions helped to establish the Trade Union movement in Great Britain.

Opposite: Another memorial plaque on the wall of the old Shire Hall, Dorchester, commemorating the 150th anniversary of the transportation of The Tolpuddle Martyrs.

GEORGE LOVELESS
THOMAS STANDFIELD
JAMES HAMMETT
JAMES LOVELESS
JOHN STANDFIELD
JAMES BRINE
By reason union justice law
We claim the birthright
We raise the watch-
ENCLOSURES

9

Fire and Water

IN THE MIDDLE AGES the risk of fire and of it spreading through a town or village unchecked was always present. Many trades such as fat renderers used open fires and were dealing with inflammable materials. Nearly all houses and cottages were huddled close together. The roofs were thatched and the walls built of cob – a mixture clay and straw, or timber. So if one roof caught fire the chances of it spreading were extremely high.

Blandford seems to have been particularly prone to devastation by fire having had conflagrations in 1676 and 1713, but the fire of 1731 left the town in ruins with all the public buildings destroyed, only forty dwellings left standing and fourteen people dead.

Opposite: This Doric Portico, known as The Fire Monument or Bastards Pump commemorates the rebuilding of Blandford.

Within thirty years the town had been completely rebuilt in the current Georgian style thanks to the efforts of John and William Bastard. These brothers, who were architects, politicians, and entrepreneurs, designed and organised the resurrection of Blandford and they are remembered in a Doric Portico erected and paid for by John Bastard in 1760.

The inscription inside The Fire Monument.

The inscriptions inside the Fire Monument read:

1768 JOHN BASTARD gave to the Bailiff and Burgesses of this town 600 pounds in trust that the Interest of 500 pounds be laid out every Year in teaching 35 Boys and Girls to read and to buy propor Books And that the Interest of the other 100 pounds be laid out in keeping this Pump in repair and supplying the Lamp with Oil and a Man to light the same every Night from Michaelmas to Lady day forever.

IN REMEMBRANCE of God's dreadful Visitation by FIRE which broke out the 4th June 1731, and in a few Hours reduced, not only the CHURCH and almost this whole Town to Ashes wherein 14 Inhabitants perished, but also two adjacent Villages And in grateful Acknowledgement of the DIVINE MERCY that has since raised this Town, like the PHÆNIX from it's Ashes to it's present beautiful and flourishing State And to prevent by a timely Supply of Water (with God's Blessing) the fatal Consequences of FIRE hereafter THIS MONUMENT of that dire Disaster and Provision against the like is humbly erected by JOHN BASTARD, a considerable Sharer in the general Calamity. 1760.

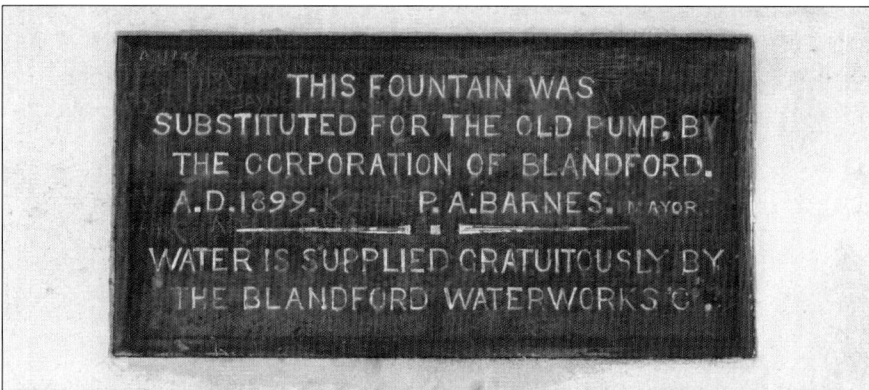

THIS FOUNTAIN WAS SUBSTITUTED FOR THE OLD PUMP, BY THE CORPORATION OF BLANDFORD. A.D.1899.   P. A. BARNES. MAYOR

WATER IS SUPPLIED GRATUITOUSLY BY THE BLANDFORD WATERWORKS C°.

The fountain is now defunct, the bowl full of litter.

Not far from Blandford in the village of Spetisbury is an old thatched cottage that has stood for at least five hundred years; although now empty, it was latterly the Marigold Tea Rooms. On the wall facing the road is a fine Sun Fire Insurance mark. This clearly identified the cottage as being insured and would probably have been placed there at around the turn of the 18th century. With the memory of the fire in Blandford still in people's minds the insurance agent would not have had a difficult task selling fire insurance.

The Sun Fire Insurance mark on a cottage wall in Spetisbury near the Woodpecker Inn.

Close-up of the Sun Fire Insurance mark in Spetisbury.

Most villages have lost their village pump but a good example from 1880 is in Iwerne Minster. The shelter over it is from a later period built by the owner of the estate at the time, James Ismay. He put it up so that the villagers could gather there and read the latest news from the front during the First World War.

In the West of the county at Thorncombe there is still a village tap that runs clear and pure. Forde Abbey had been bought in 1863 by Mrs Bertram Evans when it was in considerable disrepair. She, with her son William, did much to restore the house and estate as well as helping the people of Thorncombe. After his mother's death in 1894 he only lived for a few years but planned a water supply for the village of Thorncombe which was installed after his death as a memorial to him.

The Thorncombe village water tap. The inscription reads: *This supply of drinking water for the people of Thorncombe was planned by William Herbert Evans in whose memory it was laid in 1902.*
Opposite: The 1880 village pump in Iwerne Minster.

10

Omnium Gatherum

THIS CHAPTER IS A MEDLEY of other interesting signs with some history behind them that I have seen in my travels around Dorset.

Max Gate in Dorchester is well known as the home of Thomas Hardy but under the trees on the left as go you in is his pets' cemetery. The graves are marked with stones now stained green with age but the most famous of these is his dog called Wessex.

Wessex, a rough haired terrier, lived from 1913 to 1926. Hardy doted on him and spoiled him relentlessly but Wessex soon had a reputation for biting any visitor to Max Gate. Among his victims were John Galsworthy, Sir Frederick Treves and many others although he welcomed TE Lawrence. He was particularly

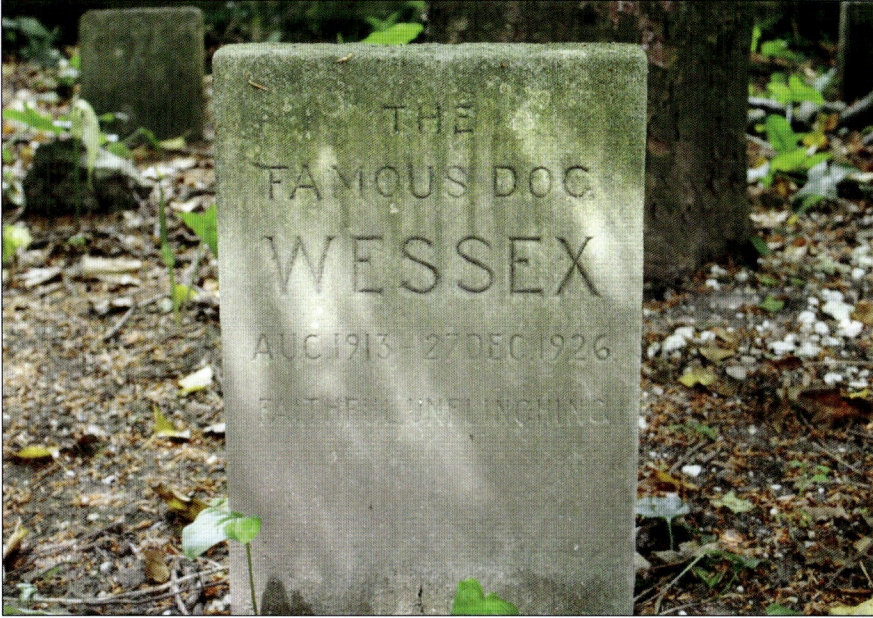

The gravestone of Thomas Hardy's dog Wessex at Max Gate, Dorchester.

aggressive towards postmen one of whom kicked out two of his teeth. He died just after Christmas 1926 his demise probably hastened by being fed goose and plum pudding at the table.

*   *   *

Just inside Charmouth churchyard is the tomb of James Warden who had a distinguished career in the Royal Navy, being a veteran of nineteen battles and numerous adventures. On his retirement from the Royal Navy he lived near Charmouth adjacent to a friend with whom he had an unfortunate quarrel. The dispute was over nothing more serious than a partridge and his friend challenged him to a duel. They met in a field near Hunter's Lodge. Warden fired first his ball going through his friend's hat. The friend's shot went through Warden's heart.

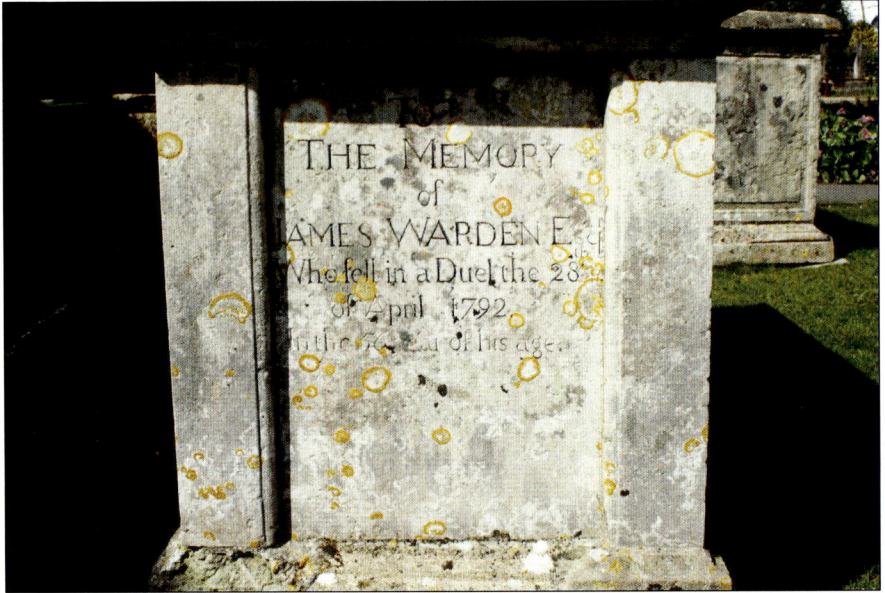

The tomb of James Warden in Charmouth churchyard who was killed in a duel over a partridge.

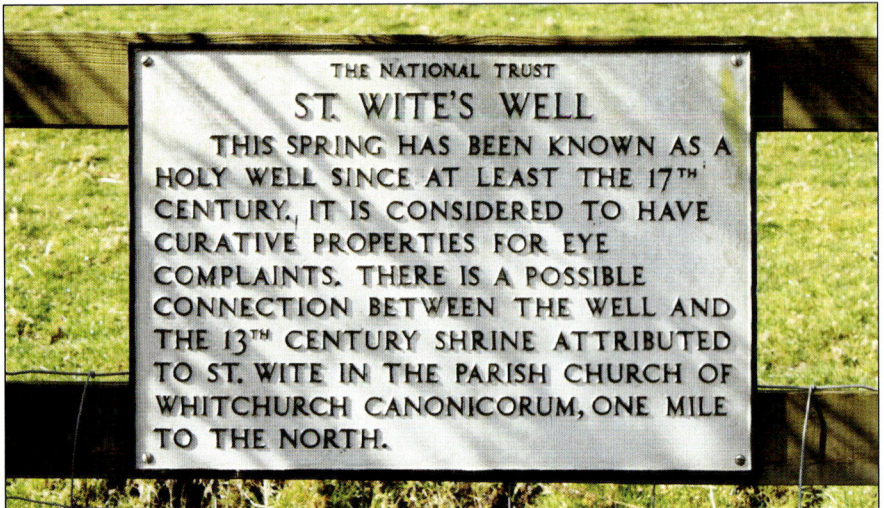

THE NATIONAL TRUST

ST. WITE'S WELL

THIS SPRING HAS BEEN KNOWN AS A HOLY WELL SINCE AT LEAST THE 17TH CENTURY., IT IS CONSIDERED TO HAVE CURATIVE PROPERTIES FOR EYE COMPLAINTS. THERE IS A POSSIBLE CONNECTION BETWEEN THE WELL AND THE 13TH CENTURY SHRINE ATTRIBUTED TO ST. WITE IN THE PARISH CHURCH OF WHITCHURCH CANONICORUM, ONE MILE TO THE NORTH.

St Wite's Well near Morecombelake.

Follow the footpath from Morecombelake to St Gabriels and Golden Cap and you pass a small fenced enclosure in which is a spring of cool fresh water. This is St Wite's Well, the water of which is reputed to have restorative qualities for the eyes.

St Wite, also known as St Candida or maybe Gwen, was a Saxon woman hermit martyred by an invading party of Danes in 831. Her shrine is in Whitchurch Canonicorum church.

*   *   *

In the Middle Ages, scurvy and similar skin complaints were very prevalent, washing and personal hygiene not being a discipline that had been invented. Scrofula, or King's Evil, was the general name for these skin diseases and custom had it that they could be cured by being touched by the king.

This sign reads: *According to tradition King Edward VI sat beneath this tree and touched for the King's Evil.*

The ancient oak tree where King Edward VI touched to cure the King's Evil.

The 'Boy King' Edward VI himself died of tuberculosis at the age of sixteen, but before this he touched people to cure them of King's Evil under a large oak tree that still stands near Woodlands.

*   *   *

Robert Whitehead was one of a crop of British engineers, inventors and entrepreneurs who flourished throughout the world in the second half of the nineteenth century. He had been making textile machinery in Milan and then moved to Fiume (now Rijeka) and was involved making and designing warships. In 1868 he sold his first successful torpedo to the Austrian Navy and soon the Royal Navy showed an interest.

He had now become wealthy and his family married into European aristocracy giving him further influence. When the Royal Navy ordered torpedoes they insisted that they be made in Great

Britain, so Whitehead established a factory on Portland harbour near Ferrybridge. He died in 1905 but the firm continued, now owned by Vickers and Armstrong-Whitworth. It grew rapidly in the two world wars but shrunk in peacetime. After World War II the company was still making torpedoes but their manufacture was moved to Swindon. The Whitehead Torpedo Factory was sold in 1989 and the site used for desirable housing.

Incidentally, in 1912 George Whitehead's great grand-daughter, Marguerite, met and married Austrian submarine commander Captain von Trapp, the father of the singing family in the Julie Andrews film "The Sound of Music". Although Whitehead received honours from many countries, his work was never recognised with any honour in Great Britain.

The original foundation stone of the Whitehead Torpedo Factory still clearly legible after nearly 120 years. Countess Hoyos was Whitehead's daughter Alice.

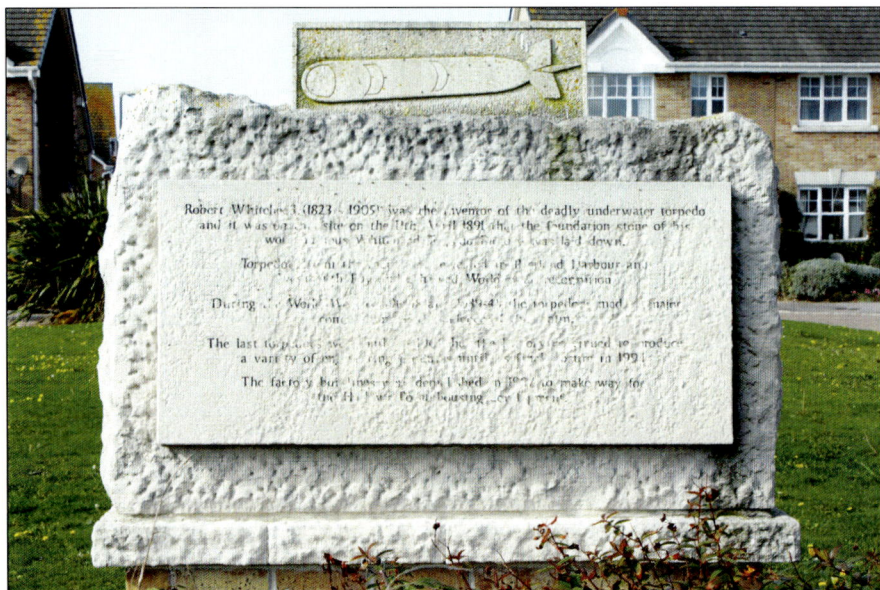

This stone tablet commemorates the Whitehead Torpedo factory. Although it is less than fifteen years old it is almost illegible. The ugly representation of a torpedo is made of cast concrete.

The inscription on this tablet reads: *Robert Whitehead (1823-1905) was the inventor of the deadly underwater torpedo, and it was on this site on 11th April 1891 that the foundation stone of his world famous Whitehead Torpedo Factory was laid down.*

Torpedoes from the Factory were tested in Portland Harbour and Weymouth Bay and achieved World wide recognition.

During the World Wars of 1914-1918 and 1939-1945 the torpedoes made a major contribution to the defence of the realm.

The last torpedoes were built in 1966 but the factory continued to produce a variety of engineering products until its final closure in 1994.

The factory buildings were demolished in 1997 to make way for the Harbour Point housing development.

Behind the Town Hall in Swanage is a fine example of a 19th century lock-up. The inscription above the door was probably put there more in hope than expectation.

The 19th century lock-up in Swanage.

Erected
For the Prevention
of
Vice & Immorality
By
The Friends of Religion & good Order
A.D. 1803.

The sign above the door on the Swanage lock-up.

In North Dorset, St Andrews church at Trent is unusual in having a steeple, but it also has a sign hanging in the church porch that encourages the congregation not to bring too much mud into the church. There is also the attractively decorated arch with mirror lettering. This may have been written in this fashion so that young ladies in the congregation peeping in their mirrors would remember that earthly beauty does not last.

This sign hangs in the porch at St Andrews church Trent and must date back at least 100 years.

The arch over the entrance to the North Chapel in Trent church. The mirror writing reads: *ALL FLESH IS GRASSE AND THE GLORY OF IT IS AS THE FLOVRE OF THE FIELDE*

Another curio in North Dorset is the oldest pillar box still in daily use in Great Britain. It is at Barnes Cross, Holwell. It was made of cast iron by John N Butt and Company of Gloucester during the 1850s. It has a small vertical slot with a flap on the inside to keep out the rain.

The Victorian letter box at Holwell is the oldest example in daily use in Great Britain.

Although having lived in Dorset for more than fifty-five years, it was not until I recently started taking photographs of plaques and signs I realised the wealth of stories that they told.

I hope this volume has brought these tales to life and will encourage, as it has in me, a deeper interest in our local history and heritage.

THE END

SOME FURTHER READING

Bellamy, Jean. *A Dorset Quiz Book*. S.B. Publications, 1995.

Bettey, J.H. *Tudors & Stuarts*. Dovecote Press, 2006.

Brown, Mary. *Dorset Customs, Curiosities and Country Lore*. Ensign Publications, 1990.

Chandler, James. *Great Characters in Dorset*. Book Guild 1991.

Cullingford, Cecil N. *A History of Dorset*. Phillimore 1980.

Dacombe, Marianne R. *Dorset Up Along and Down Along*. Dorset Federation of Womens Institutes, 1935.

Eedle, Marie de G. *The Daniels and Knowle*. The Author, 1993.

Eedle, Marie de G. *Horn Hill Tunnel*. The Author, 1994.

Guttridge, Roger. *The Villages of Dorset*. Ensign Publications, 1993.

Hutchins, John. *History and Antiquities of Dorset*. 2 volumes. Unknown, 2010.

Newman, John and Pevsner, Nikolaus. *The Buildings of England: Dorset*. Penguin, 1972

Ollard, Richard. *Dorset, Pimlico County History Guides*. Pimlico, 1995.

Osborn, George. *Dorset Curiosities*. Dovecote Press, 1986.

Viner, David. *Roads, Tracks, & Turnpikes*. Dovecote Press, 2007.

NOTES